"When you're broken on the ground,
you will be found."

"Today is going to be a good day
            and here's why..."

"Today a least you're you
and that's enough."

"You do the hard thing
  'cause that's the right thing."

"All you gotta do is just believe
you can be who you want to be."
                    Sincerely, Me

"You are **not alone**."

"No one deserves to be forgotten.
   No one deserves to disappear."

"All we see is sky for forever."

"I'm waving through a window."

"Maybe there's a reason to believe
                    you'll be okay."

"It takes a little patience,
    takes a little time."

100

"No one should stick it out
  or have any doubt that it matters
    that they are here."

"It's easy to change
        if you give it your attention."

Made in the USA
Lexington, KY
14 October 2018